"

Tell me and I forget. Teach me and I remember. Involve me and I learn.

Benjamin Franklin

THE UGLY TRUTH ABOUT LIFE INSURANCE

MIKE HARRISON

IF I ONLY KNEW...

The World is in Peril. Disease and Calamities abound. It feels as though someone put the Earth in the oven, set the temperature to 400 degrees, and walked away. The Unexpected has now become the Expected. Truly a time of concern, we are still living during a period of massive innovation and productivity. Technology has never been more advanced or more impactful. Growing up, living like "The Jetsons" seemed incredibly far off...Not Anymore.

Despite the advancements, many things have stayed the same. I don't care what medications we take, how many freezers we sleep in, what diets we consume, or what hours we spend in the gym, Death is Inevitable. This is what makes Life Insurance is a $1.1 Trillion industry. Sheesh! So What is Life Insurance? It is simply a promise that an insurer will pay a designated beneficiary a sum of money upon the death of an insured person. The earliest known written Life Insurance policy was in Royal Exchange, London in 1583. Since then over 5,000 insurance companies are now carving out a piece of the trillion-dollar pie. Let the games begin.

I have been in the Life Insurance business for the past seven years and have seen it all. There are clients on the books that I've had since my first month in business to clients I've insured- the client lost coverage, got the coverage back, and lost it again. I had a couple of clients get coverage then, a few weeks later they passed away. This business will enrich you with experiences. I walked into a house and covered the Mom and all three children, but Dad passed on it. He told me to wait a little while for his coverage. Two weeks later, he was murdered right in front of his apartment. No Insurance. There was also a gentleman I had been trying to cover for TWO YEARS. (I never quit, by the way.) One day, this gentleman got into a car accident on the highway and unfortunately was in a coma for ten days. Luckily, he survived and had all his wits. After about 30 days, I spoke with him. I was certain after his brush with death he would be begging me for a policy. He said, "Mike, I'm lucky to be alive, and I appreciate how long you have been working with me. I need Life Insurance, I just can't afford it, right now!" My man...you can't afford not to have it. If he had passed away, his daughter, who was in her 30s, would have had to come up with thousands. If this didn't convince him, I don't know what could.

Ironically, I was a Client before I became an Agent. A friend of mine from high school was selling Life Insurance and I wanted to support his business. At the time, it made sense. I was 35 years old with a Wife and three children. I was an entrepreneur with no coverage. He sold me a $1 Million 20 Year Term policy for $95/month. I was now a Millionaire. (Laugh Out Loud!) Unfortunately, there was no education during the process. All I heard was $95 and $1 Million insurance. It wasn't until I got into the business that I could distinguish between policies and what could benefit me and my clients. Knowing what I know now, I would not have signed off on that policy so quickly. I will explain this in greater detail later in the book. You live and you learn.

I want to thank you for taking the time out of your day to read this book. Today, I'm going to treat you like family. By the time you finish reading these pages, you're going to know more about Life Insurance than most Agents. With this knowledge, you will make better decisions for yourself and your family. You can Thank Me Later.

THE DAYS DRAG ON...BUT THE YEARS FLY BY

The longer you wait to get covered, the more expensive it will be. Life Insurance is not retail, and there will be no discounts. Age and health determine your life Insurance premiums, so the older and unhealthier you become, the more expensive the premiums. It amazes me how people try to avoid getting covered or get the absolute rock-bottom price possible. I hear things such as "That's ok Mike, when I die, I'm going to donate my body to science instead", or "I'm going to dig a hole in the backyard and someone can just put me in there" or "I'll hold off on the Life Insurance, I'll just get someone to set me on fire after I die" and the funniest one is "I'm going to SAVE the money for my burial instead! So let me get this straight, you just complained that you were on a fixed income and couldn't afford $50/month but now you can MIRACULOUSLY save $5000-$10,000 for your Final Expenses??? Highly unlikely. Somebody better be ready to pony up some money when you pass away.

"I Can't Die Until After Two Years!!???" I always giggle under my breath when I hear this from a senior. Potential clients love me until I tell them they are approved for coverage but approved for the graded/modified policy. A graded or modified policy is due to their questionable health and now the insurance company deems the client as a risk. These policies will pay the full-face value only after you've had the policy for at least two years. The insurance company even has the nerve to jack up the price on the premiums as well. If a client passes away before the two years, the company will "reimburse" all paid premiums in by the insured plus a percentage to the beneficiary. Clients get heated when they hear this and immediately want other options. Some of these clients have cancer and fully aware they are fighting the clock. Clients need to understand is that the fact they received approval for anything is a Win considering the severity of the health of some of them. Also, dying before the two years is the worst-case scenario. If that happens, at least the beneficiary will receive everything paid plus interest. The policy acted as a high-interest savings account which means the Life Insurance was virtually "Free." Once I explain it that way, the client usually drops their shoulders. Then I say, "After two years, Mrs. Jones, you can die all you want."

In reality, almost all Life Insurance policies have a two-year waiting period. It's called the Contestability period. Yes, you may be approved for immediate coverage, which means if you pass away within the first two years of coverage, the insurance company should pay. However, during the Contestability period, the company has the right to do a thorough investigation, including requesting medical records and checking for accuracy on the initial application. If the research doesn't match properly, they WILL NOT pay the claim. The beneficiary will only get the paid payments like the policy was approved as graded. If it was an accidental death then it's typically no issue but these insurance companies don't play. Case in point, I had an 82 year old client get a small $5000 whole life policy in August of 2018. Three months later, the client was found dead in her kitchen in what appeared to be a heart attack. With this client's age and little policy, I figured this would be a no-brainer for the company to just "cut the check." Absolutely Not. The insurance company investigated this client to the fullest. They eventually paid out the claim, in February 2019.

Someone once said, "Procrastination is the grave in which opportunity is buried." When I speak with people about getting life insurance for the first time, there is a natural tendency to put it off. They aren't quick to react, unless a person close to them has passed away, a person close to them is very sick or an insurance agent like me is irritating the crap out of them. Not reacting can cost you dearly. In November 2021, I had a conversation with a couple. Anna, a wife, was 53 years old, and Jack, her husband, was 74. Naturally the couple recognized the importance of coverage but they wanted to wait until after the holidays, so we agreed that we would touch-base in early January 2022. After several phone calls, I contacted Anna and what she told me left no room for shock in this business. In December 2021, Anna had a heart attack, and Jack was diagnosed with cancer. Within 30 days, everything changed. I insured the couple, but it had to be with an expensive "no health question" policy, which, included the 2-year waiting period. If they would have gotten the insurance when we first spoke, it would have saved them thousands of dollars. Unless there is a financial issue, GET THE INSURANCE IMMEDIATELY.

Here is a jewel for all seniors who have owned Life Insurance policies for 10-plus years. Most policies have a feature called "Reduced Paid Up." This feature will reduce the face value of your policy in exchange for no premium. Reduced paid up may be a godsend for some seniors because it could free up some money every month. This feature will only work for clients that own multiple policies or have had at least one policy for at least ten years. After reviewing your coverages, you may realize you are Over-Insured and don't need as many policies. You may have five policies with a total of $50,000 in coverage. You may decide you only need $30,000, so you reduce $25,000 to $5000. Now you have eliminated half your payments. There is also a way where the Reduced Paid Up option can give you MORE coverage for less in premium. I had a client that had a $20,000 whole life policy paying $70/month. She had this policy for 11 years. The client was struggling financially, so she asked me if any options could help her. She did not want to lose her coverage. She needed something cheaper. I shopped around for her and found a $15,000 policy for $45/month. The client thanked me, but had no interest in lowering her coverage. I told her we were going to ADD face value. We both talked to the insurance company and asked what the Reduced Paid-Up option would be on the $20K. They said $7,000, and it would eliminate her monthly premium. So we executed the Reduced Paid Up option and added the $15,000 policy. Like that, my client had $22,000 in coverage for $45/month. Problem Solved.

TERMS & CONDITIONS

As I said earlier in the book, as a client my first insurance policy was a huge-term. It was an awesome feeling to get that policy in my hands. I felt proud because if anything happened to me, my family would not have to worry and then some. When I became an agent, I discovered this couldn't be further from the truth. Don't get me wrong, term policies have their place, I sell term policies all day. Also, EVERYONE needs Life Insurance no matter how young, and sometimes term is the only affordable option. They are an excellent option for mortgage protection, Key Man business partnerships, and Church leadership as well. Now, let me break down why I draw the line right there.

There have been countless homes where I walked in, and they were outraged because they received a letter stating their premiums were to increase by $200-$300 in the next six months. Also, every year up until their 80th birthday, there will be a premium increase on their birthday. I see this with regularity in low income communities. I can picture how the scene unfolds. You are in your late 40's, maybe early 50's. An insurance agent tells you you can get $250,000 in coverage for $40/month. WHO WOULDN'T TAKE THAT? Where do I sign??? Why would you get a whole life policy at this point? Let me explain. Most likely this policy would last 20 years. The question is-what happens after 20 years? No one asks that. No one thinks about that. It's never an issue until you outlive the term. Think about this, only nine percent of term policies ever pay. This is why insurance companies can keep these policies so cheap. As a business, if I sell to 100 people and I only receive claims from 9 of them, then I'm winning all day. It's almost like 91 people are giving to charity. Term policies help the bottom line for insurance companies. Accidental policies are even worse. At least a term policy will pay in full no matter how you die but an accidental policy??? You literally have to die in an accident for it to pay the claim. Are you serious???

Let's say your term policy ends at age 71 and your payment for 20 years was $40/month. You just received a letter showing your premium is going up to $200/month on your 71st birthday. You know that this is not the time for your expenses to go up and since you are 71 years old it will be hard for you to get another term. Now you need to get a whole life policy and let's say your health is not good. This example is another factor that will make your whole-life policy more expensive (with a potential two-year wait). People never consider this. The only way the term policy was to work was if you were lucky enough to die within the term period. My recommendation to my younger clients if they are persistent about getting a term policy, is to get a small whole life alongside it. If the term runs out you still have permanent coverage. This method also applies to Life Insurance on your job. It's a group coverage term, so it's cheap. However, once you quit the job- it's a whole new ballgame. ALWAYS, ALWAYS get a policy outside of your job. It will be more expensive, but you can control it. That alone is worth the price.

IN BENEFICIARIES WE TRUST

Would you believe, for some, the hardest decision to make is deciding who their beneficiary will be? I had someone wait three months before committing to getting her Life Insurance because she couldn't decide who to leave the money. It was an agonizing decision for them. As I have spent some years in the business, I now understand the plight. Every January, 2-3 Clients call me to change their beneficiaries because someone pissed them off over the holidays. It's like musical chairs sometimes. When a Client finally passes away, people come near & far to "check in" just to confirm there is no money lying around for them. You truly see a person's character during these times. I've heard stories of people tearing a house apart to find something of value when someone has passed. Brother and sister will fistfight over Dad's 2005 Cadillac. When a person has chosen you to be their beneficiary, that is a high and prestigious honor. That means someone has thought so highly of you that they trust you to perform their last wishes. However, once that person has passed the accountability is gone. Most likely, there won't be anyone standing over your shoulder saying, "Mommy didn't say spend the money like that!" It's only you and your conscience.

Everyone please repeat after me, I WILL ALWAYS UPDATE MY LIFE INSURANCE POLICY WHENEVER THERE IS A LIFE CHANGING EVENT. We all have them. Death, divorce, childbirth, job change, mortgage paid off, etc., all qualify for life-changing events that can seriously impact who your beneficiary should be. Some Clients get additional policies when the family gets large. Most Clients do nothing. I have been in countless homes where the beneficiary still reads the FORMER Spouse. Many have been remarried, for years, but they never updated the policy. Not realizing that, after their death, their current spouse will not get a dime of that Life Insurance. Case in point, one of the most egregious acts I've seen was about four years ago. A Client, let's call him Bill, moved to Connecticut from North Carolina to be with his girlfriend. Bill was 59 years old at the time. Things didn't work out as planned while in Connecticut. Not only did the relationship end, but he also got severely ill. He ended up moving back to North Carolina and living with his brother. Within a year, Bill was dead. His brother found Bill's Life Insurance policy. The good news was the insurance policy was worth $100,000. The bad news was the ex-girlfriend in Connecticut was the beneficiary. The odds of his family getting this money were slim but they needed funds to put Bill in the ground. After several attempts, Bill's brother contacted her and had a funds conversation. He might as well have been talking to a wall. She was stern and said she was not going to contribute a dime to Bill's burial. She said, and I quote, "That's on y'all."

Also: Please refrain from having anyone under 18 years old listed as a beneficiary. If you pass away and the child is still under age, you may have created a massive headache. First, if the child is unaware of the policy, who will help the child complete the paperwork to get the money? Second, let's say the Life Insurance company sends the check to the child, how will the child cash the check? They will need a bank account in their name, or there needs to be a Guardian in place. This ordeal may take months. Do everyone a favor. Always have someone of age as a beneficiary and give them specific instructions on the distribution of funds. Once the child or children are of age, then change the beneficiaries. I know this is tough, but when you set up Life Insurance, set it up like you're dying next week. It needs to be as detailed as possible so there are no issues. Also, if someone is a beneficiary PLEASE TELL THEM. There is $7.4 Billion in unclaimed Life Insurance money. I think a big part of this is because people are unaware that Grandma left them $10,000! Don't keep life insurance a secret. Let your loves know you care about them enough to leave something behind.

THE GRASS AIN'T ALWAYS GREENER

November 9, 1989, the Berlin Wall came down. This event ushered in the Information Age. The World has never been the same. We went from pay phones and LAN lines to pagers, to fax machines, to email, to blackberries, to cell phones, to smartphones to self-driving cars to flying cars all within 30 years. Knowing your Wi-fi passcode is as vital as knowing your social security number. Who would have thought our cell phones would also be our personal computers? Information comes and goes at breakneck speed, and consumers have access to everything. The information highway also includes price comparisons with insurance companies. This method has become a gift and a curse. I can do business with someone, and within 30 minutes, they can call me back and say they found something cheaper.

Ladies and gentlemen, please be very careful about canceling or replacing policies. I don't recommend it at all. I totally understand saving money, but it could be to your detriment. Remember, every new policy is a fresh contestability period. Also, when you change policies it should be apples to apples. I've had Clients call and say that they canceled their whole-life and got a term-policy because it was more insurance for a lower price. OMG. I melt in sadness when I hear these things. Even worse, someone will say that they canceled their policy because someone from another company QUOTED them a cheaper price. No underwriting, no approval, just a quote. You got to be kidding me. I spoke with a gentleman on the phone a couple of weeks ago who was looking for coverage. He said he already had a policy but was no longer going to pay it because he didn't like the fact that it had a two-year waiting period. He wanted a policy with immediate coverage. I said, "If you have a two-year waiting period, there must be some health concerns." He said, "I'm on dialysis." I responded, "Sir, you're lucky to have a policy. I recommend bringing your policy current so it won't lapse." He said, "I'll take my chances."

In March last year, Sherry called me and said she wanted more affordable coverage. She had her current policy for only about a month with another company. I was able to offer her about $4000 more in coverage for about $20 less per month, and she accepted. You guessed it, about a month and a half later, she called me and said someone knocked on her door and offered her a policy of $20 cheaper than what she received from me and was considering replacing the policy. I told her, "Sherry if you switch now this will be the third company you've had in three months. There will always be someone cheaper. At some point, you gotta make a commit." She respected what I said, stuck with me, and she's been my Client since.

If you are going to replace your coverage, I recommend doing this. First, get the approval for the new policy and set the first payment about 30 days out. If you have cash in the original insurance policy, surrender it or exercise the Reduced Paid up option. If not, call the company and take the insurance off the automatic bank draft. DO NOT CANCEL IT. Have them bill you directly. In 30 days, you will start paying the new policy, and you're all good. So, what happens to the old policy? It will eventually cancel out due to nonpayment, that will take some time. Let me explain why I recommend doing it this way. I had a Client replace his policy, but he canceled the original one. Unfortunately, he passed away less than three months after this happened. If he hadn't canceled the original insurance policy, it would still be active, and his beneficiaries could have gotten payment from both companies. Timing is everything.

GENERATIONAL WEALTH

We live in a world where whoever controls the Gold controls everything. No matter your beliefs, you can say money isn't everything, but try surviving a couple weeks without it. Money controls EVERYTHING. For those who disagree, keep living. Most of us will work for at least 40 years, hope we have a healthy retirement account (401K, 403b, TSP, etc), and live the remainder of our years on social security and/or pension. Some of us are also proverbial entrepreneurs. We will go our entire lives building a passive income that we can hopefully pass down from generation to generation. People fail to realize is that there is a foolproof plan to finance all future generations. Yes, Life Insurance. It can start with you, TODAY.

You don't have to build a million-dollar company to pass down, you don't have to hope and pray, and there doesn't have to be any scamming going on. You can blaze the trail to financial freedom for as little as $20-per month. Let me explain. There are what they call Increased Death Benefit policies or Level B universal life policies. These policies are expensive for most adults but for those under 18 years old, these policies are very inexpensive. The policies work like this. A typical policy, let's say a $30,000 universal or whole life will always be $30,000 whether you have had it one year or 30 years. Well, a $30,000 Level B policy will start at $30,000, but in 30 years the policy may be worth $120,000. The policy's value increases yearly (hence the increased-death benefit policy). If you have a child or grandchild that is one year old, 5-years old, 10-years old, etc. will be perfect. Imagine getting a $100,000 policy for a one-year old and how much value that policy would have in 40 years. This child could use some of the cash, also (I'll get more in-depth about these policies in another book). If we teach our children and grandchildren the power of Life Insurance and they make it a habit to get it and KEEP it, it will create generational wealth instantly. After someone dies, a beneficiary is blessed with 6 to

7 figures tax-free. We may not benefit from it today, but our great-grands would thank you immensely.

Appropriately used, Life Insurance is power. There is a misconception that the Wealthy do not need to purchase it. Why would they? They have more money in their socks than in our bank accounts. Did you know a wealthy Tech businessman owns the largest Life Insurance policy to date? It is a $212 Million policy with an annual premium of $6.1 Million. Why would a millionaire own a Life Insurance policy? It's because he understands that the value added would be much more substantial than cash on hand. He has it figured out. Do you???

CONCLUSION

In America alone, there are 102 Million people who have no Life Insurance or are underinsured. According to Worldometers.info, at the time of this writing, there have been 110 Million births and 50 Million deaths so far this year worldwide. When you look at the many insurances we have to purchase during our lifetime, Health insurance, Renters insurance, Critical Illness, Car Insurance, Homeowners, Long Term Care, Dental, Vision, etc., there is only one we are guaranteed to use-Life. I get it, though. Sometimes, I don't trust insurance companies. If I get in a car accident are they going to pay? You pay your premiums every month for years, and when something happens, it seems like the insurance company is finding every reason in the world NOT to pay. Suddenly the fine print becomes BOLD when you expect a claim to be settled. I get it because I've been there. Honestly, concerning Life Insurance, if the premiums are up to date and the policy has been in effect for at least two years, there should be no problems. Not even suicide will stop that claim from being paid. A record $100 Billion was paid out in Life Insurance claims in 2021. Somebody, somewhere, knows how to properly fill out paperwork.

For those of you who have no Life Insurance, are underinsured, or are interested in the Increased Death Benefit policy do not hesitate to reach out to me. I can also assist with Medicare, the Market Place, and Financial Planning. You are the most important investment you can make. I would like to Thank you for your purchase, and hope you are more educated now than before you read the book. Remember, knowledge is knowledge, but Applied knowledge is life changing.

Mike Harrison

Phone# 919-925-0842

Email: mike@4eversuccess.com

IG: mikedainsuranceguy

Web: mikeharrisontheinsuranceguy.com

Mikeharrison.club

www.ingramcontent.com/pod-product-compliance
Lightning Source LLC
Chambersburg PA
CBHW050528290526
45786CB00007B/2743